SPACE AND SOCIETY 1
THE REGION

SPACE AND SOCIETY 1

THE REGION

Andrew Kirby and David Lambert

LONGMAN

LONGMAN GROUP LIMITED
Longman House
Burnt Mill, Harlow, Essex CM20 2JE, England
and Associated Companies throughout the world.

First published 1984
ISBN 0 582 35356 4

Set in 10/11pt Baskerville, Linotron 202

Printed in Singapore by
The Print House (Pte) Ltd

Contents

Preface   vii

1 Regions and natural areas   1

  1.1 What is a region?   1
  1.2 Levels of living in England and Wales   4
  1.3 Natural regions in geography   7
  1.4 Summary   11

2 Socially-made regions   13

  2.1 Regions with changing boundaries   13
  2.2 Regions that overlap   19
  2.3 A problem of local government reorganisation   21

3 Perceptual regions and mental maps   25

  3.1 Perception   25
  3.2 Barriers to perception   27
  3.3 Residential location: where people live   29
  3.4 Residential location: where people work   31

4 Drawing boundaries   35

  4.1 National and international boundaries   35
  4.2 A cultural–linguistic divide in Wales   40
  4.3 Resolving boundary disputes   46

5 Conclusions   54

Photographic section   57

Appendix   66

References   68

Acknowledgements

We are grateful to the following for permission to reproduce copyright material:

Harper and Row Ltd for an extract from pp. 138–40, *The Two Germanies* by R. H. Mellor; The Institute of British Geographers for an extract from 'Spatial Variations in Level of Living in England and Wales' by P. Knox, *Transactions*, issue 62, 1974.

We are grateful to the following for permission to reproduce photographs:

Bostock Penman and Sharpe, page 63; Camera Press, pages 60 and 65; Oxford Mail, page 61; Milton Keynes Development Corporation, page 64.

Artwork reference permission was granted by the following:

Darby, *Historical Geography of Britain before 1600*, Cambridge University Press, page 14; Dyfed Rural Council, *Pembrokeshire Historian no 4*, copyright B. S. John, page 40; David Keeble, *Industrial Location and Planning in the UK*, Methuen & co Ltd, pages 15, 16, 17 and 18; P. L. Knox, *Transactions* no 62 page 14 and *Area* 1980, vol 12 no 1, Institute of British Geographers, pages 5 and 17; Kyerematen, *Interstate Boundary Litigation in Ashanti*, Cambridge University Press 1971, page 47; Roy E. Mellor, *The Two Germanies – A Modern Geography*, Harper and Row, 1978, page 36; D. C. Money, *Climate Soils and Vegetation*, University Tutorial Press 1972, pages 8 and 9; James A. Taylor, Methods of Soil Study, *Geography 45*, page 10.

Preface

To the teacher

Aims

This series is designed for use within the sixth form as a back-up to the now familiar texts such as Tidswell's *Pattern and Process in Human Geography*, Bradford and Kent's *Human Geography* and Haggett's *Modern Synthesis*. We have designed the books as 'readers', that is, free-standing volumes that elaborate on particular topics, fleshing out the bare bones introduced within the textbook by presenting extracts from original sources and illustrative exercises. The latter are particularly important, as the emphasis throughout the series is upon the practical application of ideas, models and theories, rather than the abstract discussion of such deductive concepts. In this sense, the aim is to use the student's existing experiences of the 'real world' as a foundation for investigation, in order that these can be channelled into a systematic understanding of basic geographic principles.

Organisation

This book can be used in three ways. It is intended for use as a whole; in other words, the student should be able to use both the practical material and the original extracts in approaching a particular topic. In some instances, however, this may not be required. In such cases, it should be possible to use the practical examples alone or, if required, the published extracts as reference material.

Within each volume, a standard format is used. The authors' text is interspersed with secondary material, and at the end of each section there are questions, a check-list and notes which are designed to highlight the key issues that have been introduced. The latter are referred to throughout the text.

To the student

This book is one of a series of geography 'readers'. This means that
the aim of the series is not to provide a complete source of facts and
information for your sixth-form course; instead the intention is to
provide a firm grounding in some of the fundamental ideas within
the subject.

You should aim to read the volumes in the series as a back-up to
your course. If you have problems in understanding some sections,
discuss them with your teacher. There are, however, check-lists of
key issues at the end of each chapter which you should refer to, and
many of the ideas will become clearer as you work through the
examples.

1
Regions and natural areas

1.1 What is a region?

In simple terms, geography is about three things. First, it deals with where things are, and explanations for these locations – what is where, and why? The types of examples that you will have studied may well have included the distribution of shops, which can be explained in terms of economic factors such as accessibility. Secondly, it considers how phenomena are related to each other, for example, the ways in which estate agents tend to be found near building societies in our towns and cities. Estate agents and building societies are in the same line of work, that is, selling houses. People who buy houses need mortgages and so estate agents will often recommend their customers to nearby building societies, who lend them the funds they require. Other firms are also involved; solicitors are involved in the transactions, and they too are to be found in the vicinity.

The third aspect is the one which we are going to concentrate upon here, the ways in which phenomena interrelate to create regions. To take the examples used above a little further, we can identify in most cities groups of particular land-uses, such as the shopping centre, the commercial district, the industrial areas. Each of these constitutes a REGION.

The important point to remember at this stage is that these types of regions are ideas, not real places with rigid boundaries. If we walk around the city centre, there are no lines which mark out the edge of the commercial 'region'. The boundaries are our own creation, designed to help us to *classify* different groups of activities. (There are of course other types of regions that have well-defined boundaries – countries for example. We shall come to this in Chapter 4.)

CLASSIFICATION is important to all types of studies, although various subjects approach this topic in different ways. Earth scientists have classified geological time into eras (the Quaternary) and periods (the Pleistocene). Natural scientists employ a whole series of classifications; they distinguish between, for example, plants and animals, while within the latter there are smaller and more specific groupings such as mammals, birds or reptiles. Even within the mammals group, the classification is not perfect; there are several species which do not conform ideally to one or the other. The duck-billed platypus, for example, lays eggs (which is not typical of mammals) and yet suckles its young (which is highly unusual for reptiles and birds).

In this kind of situation, we compromise. The platypus shows more of the features of a mammal than of any other type of animal; consequently, the similarities outweigh the differences, and we are justified in calling it a mammal. From this we can build up a definition of a classification as a group in which the members have more in common with each other than they do with those outside the group.

Geography too employs methods of classification (or *taxonomy*, as it is sometimes called). It attempts to distinguish between different types of landforms, and classifies climates into 'polar', 'temperate' and 'tropical'. Human geographers try to allocate settlements to different groups, calling them 'towns', or 'villages' on the basis of their different attributes such as various types of shopping facilities. An alternative approach would be to categorise them on the basis of their primary function (market town, mining settlement, port) or their housing stock (large proportions of council houses, or large numbers of flats).

These are all ASPATIAL classifications. By this we mean that the location of the towns is not considered. However, geographers are also very concerned with SPATIAL taxonomy, which is a process of finding similar places in order to build up regions. We can illustrate this quite easily with a practical example.

Figure 1.1 is a map of the Regional Health Authorities (RHA), which are the areas by which the National Health Service is administered. For each region, the *standardised mortality ratio* is displayed. Although this sounds complicated, it is a simple statistic that relates the numbers of deaths to the numbers we would expect, given the age of the population and the balance of males to females that it has. The ratio ranges around 100, which is the average for the country as a whole.

If we were interested in analysing this map, we might attempt to simplify the problem. We could search for above- and below-average mortality, for example; which RHAs fall into which category? More importantly, is there a pattern to be seen? If there is, it is likely that neighbouring places have the same ratios because there is a common factor at work in both of them.

Looking at figure 1.1 closely, we can see that there is a pattern, and that we can build up regions of similar RHA areas. There are *three* regions, in which each RHA area shows more similarity to its neighbour than to other areas. The first region is of above-average

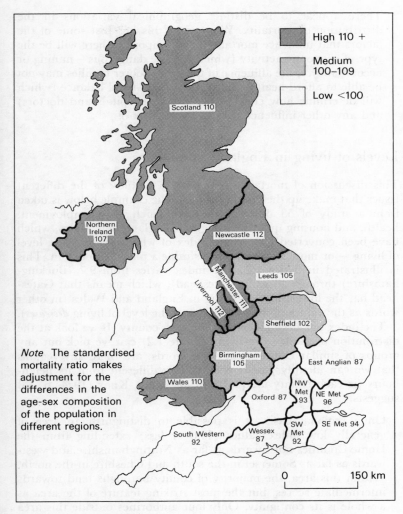

High 110 +

Medium
100–109

Low <100

Scotland 110

Northern
Ireland
107

Newcastle 112

Manchester 111

Leeds 105

Liverpool 112

Sheffield 102

Note The standardised
mortality ratio makes
adjustment for the
differences in the
age-sex composition
of the population in
different regions.

Birmingham
105

East Anglian 87

Wales 110

Oxford 87

NW
Met
93

NE Met
96

SW
Met
92

SE Met 94

South Western
92

Wessex
87

0   150 km

Figure 1.1   Standardised mortality ratios in different Regional Health Authorities

mortality, and contains those places with ratios above 110. The
second is of below-average mortality, and contains those RHA
areas with ratios below 100. The third contains intermediate ratios.
between 100 and 110.

1. Sketch figure 1.1, and draw the three regions of mortality. Try
   to find a geographical (such as 'north' or 'south') name to
   describe each region.

2. There appear to be distinct geographical variations in the distribution of mortality. Why might this be? List some of the factors that influence mortality rates: important here will be the type of economic activity (which is more dangerous – mining or accountancy?), the affluence of the area (poorer families may not be able to afford healthy diets), the urban–rural balance (which will determine how close people live to hospitals and doctors) and any other influence that you can think of.

1.2 Levels of living in England and Wales

This discussion of mortality brings us to a study of the different issues that make up the 'quality of life'. The example below is taken from a study of 53 different measures such as unemployment, health, and housing quality throughout England and Wales, which have been converted to a single index of what is called 'the level of living' – or more simply, how desirable a place is to live in. This is illustrated in figure 1.2. The index varies from 9.7 (Buckinghamshire) through to 83.9 (Gateshead), which means that Gateshead has the lowest level of living in England and Wales (in other words as the values of the index *increase*, the level of living *decreases*).

The index has been calculated for each county. If we look at the distribution of the level of living (figure 1.2) can we pick out any groups of similar counties (in other words, are there any regions that we can identify?) or is each county different from its neighbours (is each county unique?). In his study, Knox (1974, p. 15) suggests:

> On a regional basis, it is possible to distinguish an area of generally low index values (40.0 or less) extending from the Home Counties northwards as far as Nottinghamshire and westwards as far as Somerset in the south and Cheshire in the north. Within this area, the majority of county boroughs tend towards intermediate scores, but the most striking feature of the area as a whole is its contiguity. Only four authorities outside this area have values of less than 40.0: Westmorland, the North Riding of Yorkshire, York and Eastbourne. The lowest index values are found in administrative counties which both possess large areas of prosperous agricultural activity and contain many suburbs and satellite towns which are centred on the larger and more prosperous industrial and commercial cities. It is suggested therefore that the basic reasons for such low index values may be regarded as two-fold: (a) economic structure, and (b) the urban process, particularly suburbanisation. The influence of both factors has already been noted in relation to the spatial expression of the components.

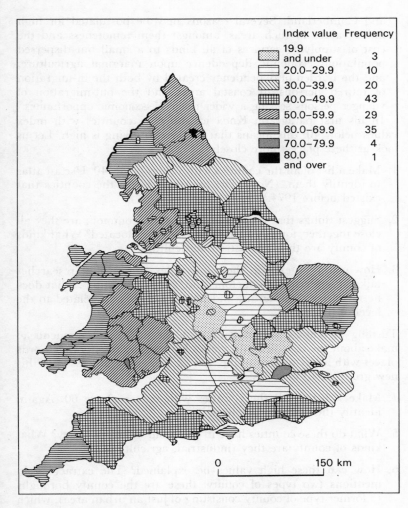

Index value	Frequency
19.9 and under	3
20.0–29.9	10
30.0–39.9	20
40.0–49.9	43
50.0–59.9	29
60.0–69.9	35
70.0–79.9	4
80.0 and over	1

0   150 km

Figure 1.2   Levels of living in England and Wales

At the other extreme, two different sorts of area can be distinguished with high index values (60.0 or more). The most numerous of these are northern industrial county boroughs, amongst which the highest scores of all are recorded and in which the legacy of the inter-war depression combined with a continued decline in the coalmining, shipbuilding and textile industries are reflected in the index values. The second type of area is constituted by a group of administrative counties, in particular by those in western Wales, but including Cornwall and Cumberland. Several reasons may be postulated for high index values in such areas, amongst them remoteness and the cost of supplying services of all kinds to a small but dispersed population: economic dependence upon marginal agriculture; and the burden of dependency created by both the in-migration of retired persons to coastal areas and the out-migration of younger persons seeking a wider range of economic opportunites.*

In his first paragraph Knox identifies 33 counties with index values below 40; this means that the level of living is high. Let us look at these places more closely.

1. Make a list of all the counties with values below 40. Use an atlas to identify them. (Note: The figures relate to the counties that existed before 1974.)

2. Suggest things that these counties have in common; are they all close together, for example? Where are they located? What kinds of county are they (industrial, agricultural)?

3. How could we explain these low index values? The researcher talks about 'economic factors' and 'suburbanisation': what does he mean by these terms, and how could they be related to the level of living?

Turning to Knox's second paragraph, he has some comments· to make about the counties with values higher than 60, in other words places with a low quality of life. Let us repeat the process with this new group of 40 counties.

4. Make a list of all the counties with values above 60. Again, identify the counties involved.

5. What do these counties have in common? Where are they? What kinds of county are they (industrial, agricultural)?

6. How can these high values be explained? The extract again mentions two types of county: these are the county boroughs (a former type of county consisting of just an urban area), which are old and economically depressed, and the rural areas on the periphery of the county. Why should these have a low level of living?

Discussion

This example sets out to investigate a fairly complicated idea, namely the differences in the level of living in England and Wales. At first glance, the pattern is complicated, but when we come to

*The full details of the source of this, and other quotations, can be found in the alphabetical list of references at the end of the book.

try to make sense of figure 1.2, we can use a rule of thumb to pick out the following: (a) the central and southeastern region of high levels of living; (b) the peripheral rural regions of low levels of living; and (c) the northern county boroughs with a low level of living. The remaining areas, with scores between 40 and 59 could be described as areas with an average quality of life.

There are pitfalls here, and an important one is CONTIGUITY, that is, whether or not all the areas are next to each other, building up into large regions. It would be possible to shade the high level of living area as a large patch on the map, but this would exclude a large block in North Yorkshire. Similarly, we could identify a large ring-shaped region with high values surrounding the core, although the county boroughs are of course all widely-scattered 'islands', with even higher values.

The danger here is that we try to force places together to make artificial regions. We have, in fact, identified *four* types of area: counties with successful industries (say, in the Midlands); wealthy counties of suburbs (such as those around London); counties containing the old industrial centres, and rural counties with poor, upland agriculture. This is a useful classification, but it is impossible to shade four distinct regions onto the map (regions, it will be remembered, have to contain *contiguous* parts).

We are left therefore with a problem, one which often faces the geographer. We have defined regions as areas more like each other than other areas. On that basis, we could just identify two big regions, a core and a periphery. We need to remember that really we have four types of area, but that these are not contiguous; they are not always next to each other, and they do not make up regions, unless we settle for a large number of little areas. It might be interesting to study these, but the aim of classification is to highlight the differences between things, and the more categories we have, the more difficult this becomes. (As an illustration of this, try to explain succinctly the difference between sports that involve a ball, and those that do not. Easy? Now try to explain in the same number of words the difference between soccer, rugby union, rugby league, hockey, steeplechasing, long-jumping, and so on.)

Four types of county, or two regions – which do you think is the most useful to the geographer trying to understand the quality of life in Britain?

1.3 Natural regions in geography

The last example, then, reveals a major problem with the use of regions: on the one hand they are a classificatory device, designed to simplify understanding, on the other, they must not be so gener-

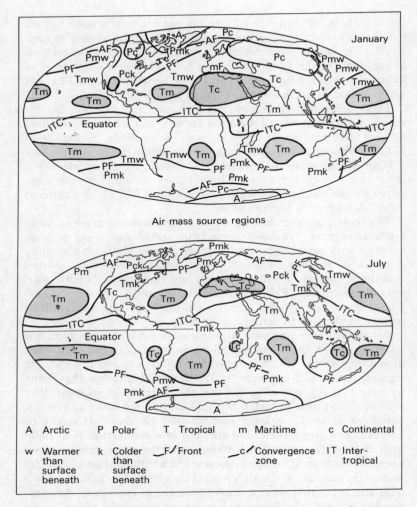

Air mass source regions

A	Arctic	P	Polar	T	Tropical	m	Maritime	c	Continental
w	Warmer than surface beneath	k	Colder than surface beneath	F / Front		c / Convergence zone		IT	Inter-tropical

Figure 1.3   The major air mass source regions and transitional zones. Shaded areas = tropical air masses

alised as to be meaningless, or so small as to be too numerous and unmanageable. As a result of this tension, geographers have always walked a tightrope between the use of regions that are large and which thus contain a great deal of internal variation, and a multitude of tiny, unique regions that bog us down in a wealth of detail.

We can see this most clearly in the fields of climatology, soils and vegetation. If we want to understand the global pattern of climate, for example, we turn to a map such as figure 1.3. This indicates

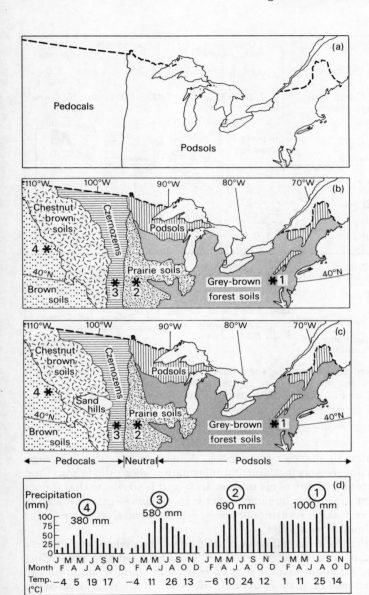

Figure 1.4   a) *Broad soil belts*
   b) *Zonal soil variation within the very broad belts*
   c) *Zonal soil variation with a major intrazonal addition – a special soil owing its attributes to parent rock rather than to broad climatic controls*
   d) *Climatic data for stations 1–4. (Approximately 40°N)*

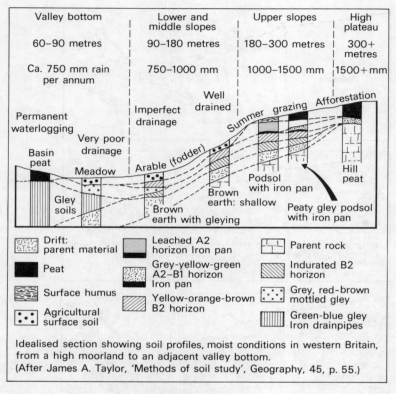

Figure 1.5   Soil variations across a valley transect

the major air mass source regions. A map such as this, although it is basic, gives us fundamental information about the origins, and therefore the nature of air masses. In fact, it is so coarse that it does not even show clear boundaries between regions – instead it simply shows very large transitional zones, which themselves extend over many hundreds of miles.

In other contexts, this type of map would be useless; in fact there are many situations in which it would be wholly misleading because we might assume that there is more climatic uniformity in a source region than is actually the case. This is illustrated by figure 1.4, which deals with the relationships between simple climatic variables and broad soil zones, in the northeastern United States. We are dealing here with types of soils that reflect different climatic factors: for example in the west, the pedocals are the product of a drier regime than is to be found in the east, where podsols are the product of more humid conditions. As figure 1.4(a) shows, even within a relatively small part of the continent, climatic differences produce two main soil types. However, even this is not the whole story. In figure 1.4(b), we can go further, and divide our two soil regions into a series of smaller zones, each of which is a response to different rainfall regimes. Finally, in figure 1.4(c) there is an additional region, termed an 'intra-zonal soil', which coincides with geological conditions in the Black Hills of Dakota. This reminds us that occasionally lithological factors are important enough for an additional type of region to be superimposed upon the underlying pattern.

These maps show us that as we try to be more and more precise in our description, then our regions have to get smaller and smaller, in order to be able to cope with greater detail. We illustrate this with our final example, which reminds us that even within our different soil regions, great local variation will occur. Figure 1.5 shows the variations in climate, soil and vegetation that result from localised factors such as relief and drainage within our broad regions. Such local variations will be widespread; however if we took them into consideration, the broad underlying patterns would be lost. Nonetheless, for someone like a farmer, these micro-regions are crucial.

1.4 Summary

This chapter has tried to explain why geographers often try to divide up the earth's surface, and what the pitfalls of this are. Regions are useful as a spatial classification; they highlight different processes happening in different areas. The aim of this classification is also important: depending upon our interests, we are likely to use very large regions, or sometimes very small ones; each has its advantages, and its disadvantages.

So far, we have concentrated upon regions as the tools of our trade. In Chapter 2 we will turn to regions that are used in everyday life.

Key issues

CLASSIFICATION All subjects deal with so much information that they have to package it into manageable proportions. Music, for example, can be classified into classical, rock, jazz and so on. In science, we divide elements up according to the periodic table, and you can no doubt think of many more examples.

SPATIAL; ASPATIAL Simply, the adjective relating to space. A spatial perspective is one that takes geographical issues into consideration – *where* things are. Aspatial is the opposite of spatial.

REGION The definition we have used in this chapter is that it is an area, in which the things enclosed have more in common with each other than they do with those outside. The 'things' in question of course vary depending upon what we are studying.

CONTIGUITY The dictionary defines contiguous as 'adjoining' or 'adjacent'. Contiguity thus exists when areas are joined.

DEGREE OF GENERALISATION This simply means the level of detail. We could apply the term to different scales of maps, for example. A 1:50,000 map is more generalised than a 1:25,000 map.

2
Socially-made regions

2.1 Regions with changing boundaries

G. H. Dury, in his book *The British Isles* (1978, p. 212) writes:
The word *region* originally meant an area subject to a single governing authority. Its meaning, that is to say, was wholly political. In the course of the natural evolution of language, the original meaning has been greatly modified – indeed, it has been almost lost, for *region* in everyday speech has no precise significance.

This quotation reminds us that for many, many years we have organised our territory into regions for political and administrative purposes. For example, figure 2.1 illustrates the existence of the several small kingdoms that were well established in the years before the Norman Conquest. In contrast to some of our previous examples, this of course means that we are dealing here with regions that do have very definite boundaries, and sometimes even guarded frontiers.

This example is also useful because it introduces the important idea that regions are not static and unchanging, but are in fact dynamic and constantly undergoing alteration in response to various factors. Political regions were originally very small. The Greeks, for example, governed themselves in city states, because poor communications precluded larger organisations. By the time of the Anglo-Saxon kingdoms, such larger units were feasible, and of course with the arrival of the Normans, England became a single, unified political entity. As society has grown more complex, administrative regions have tended to change with even greater speed. Figures 2.2(a)–(d) illustrate this. Each map represents the *assisted areas* at different dates. These regions are identified by the government as localities with concentrated economic problems (like unemployment). Within these areas, different types of financial aid are available from the government to bring about economic development. Let us look more closely at figure 2.2 and try to explain the different regions that we can see.

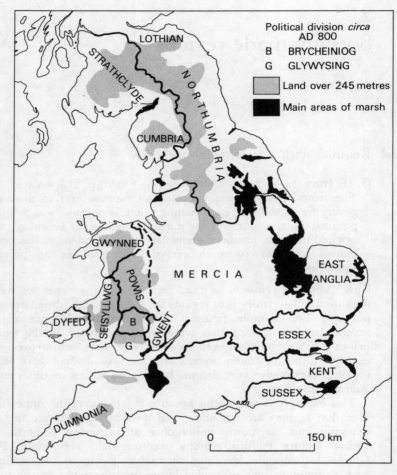

Figure 2.1   Political boundaries in England and Wales in the Anglo-Saxon era

Figure 2.2   a) *Regional aid 1934–45*

1. *Fig. 2.2 (a)* These regions were first established in 1938. They were quite small, and concentrated around specific types of area. Identify these areas, and try to explain why they were suffering from economic problems. You should try to identify the main industrial activity associated with each area.

Incentives similar
to those in the
development areas
were available in
Northern Ireland

0   150 km

b) Regional aid 1945–60

2. *Fig. 2.2* (*b*) The special areas have changed their names to
   development areas, and grown in size. Identify the localities that
   have been added to the map. Are they the same type of industrial area as those in map (a)? Again, try to identify the main
   industrial or economic activity associated with the different
   areas.

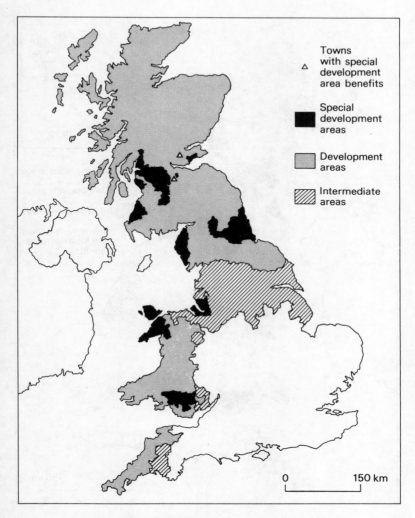

c) Regional aid 1966–75

3. *Fig. 2.2* (*c*) Again, an expansion has occurred. A hierarchy of problems is identified, with some areas receiving special development status, and others a lower grading in the form of intermediate area status. Once more, try to identify the types of places that belong to each category – do they have the same sort of economic background?

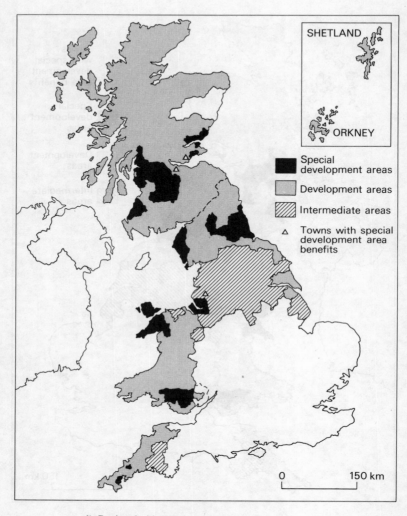

d) Regional aid 1979

4. *Fig. 2.2* (*d*) The last map shows the changed pattern of 1979, and reminds us that regional BOUNDARIES may be a *political* decision as much as a geographical one. Was it a change of government or was it an improvement in economic performance that resulted in these smaller regions?

Discussion

There are some general points that you will have already noticed – that at its greatest extent, the assisted areas policy covered the whole of northern England, Scotland, Wales and the southwest peninsula. This left only a small proportion of the United Kingdom without any development status ('non-scheduled areas'), because in addition to areas receiving aid, the southeast and the Midlands were scheduled as 'overgrowth areas' in which industrial development was actively discouraged. It is interesting to relate this to our earlier discussion concerning the level of living in the United Kingdom. If we turn back, for example, to figure 1.1, we can see that counties with low index values (high level of living) are located within this 'overgrowth' region (but why is London an exception to this generalisation?).

On a more detailed level, it is useful to compare this example with the ones used in Chapter 1, where we talked about the importance of the size and the degree of generalisation of regions. The changes in the assisted areas, between for example, maps (b) and (c), show that it was not possible to treat all areas with economic problems in the same way, and that consequently different problems had to be treated as different types of regions, which were therefore smaller and more specific.

2.2 Regions that overlap

Economic regions are the most recent type of SOCIALLY-MADE REGION. Other types of administrative regions, on the other hand, are long-established. It is no exaggeration to suggest that nearly all the aspects of government and administration with which we

Table 2.1 Spatial organisation at different scales

Activity	Organisation
Medicine	Regional ⎫ Health Authorities Area ⎭
Education	Local Education Authorities (Counties and Metropolitan districts)
Council housing	District Councils
Power	Gas and Electricity Boards
Water	Water Authorities
Railways	Regions

come into contact have some spatial basis to their organisation. This fact is underlined in table 2.1, which shows the ways in which some everyday services are organised.

One of the important points demonstrated by Table 2.1 is that many of these administrative regions operate at very different SPATIAL SCALES. (Why is this? Why should water authorities be organised as very large units, while education is provided for relatively smaller, more local areas?) This in turn means that they may not even share the same boundaries. We can examine this very simply in the following way.

1. Using your local telephone directory, prepare maps of the following:
   (a) Your local telephone area (this is presented at the front of the volume).
   (b) Your local gas board area (see under 'G').
   (c) Your local electricity board area (see under 'E').
   (d) Your local water authority (see under 'W').

2. Compare the names of the four administrative regions. Are they in any way similar?

3. Compare the boundaries of the four maps – where do they coincide, and where do they become OVERLAPPING BOUNDARIES?

4. Look at the sub-divisions within these regions. Imagine you are a householder with an emergency problem, say, that a telephone engineer has dug down – and through – the gas, water and electricity supply lines and cables. How many different places would you have to contact in your area in order to get in touch with each of these services? Is it possible to find on the maps above some locations where a householder would have to contact four entirely different places?

Discussion

This exercise should make it clear that the organisation of space is rarely perfect. The incident outlined (in number 4) is clearly unlikely, nevertheless it should not be hard to find some places in your local area that would be forced to contact widely scattered area headquarters, which could make the coordination of such services difficult. Nor are these services by any means the only ones that an individual might need to contact. Not only might gas bills, electricity bills and water rates all come from different offices, but visits to social services, housing departments and hospitals could involve journeys in entirely different directions. (Could these problems of spatial organisation be a contributory cause of many people's dislike of bureaucracies?)

.3 A problem of local government reorganisation

The whole question of the relationship between places and administrative centres has been critically examined by the government; this brought about major changes in local government organisation in 1974 (before this date, the boundaries were those shown in figure 1.2). This reorganisation resulted in the introduction of new *counties*, and within them, *districts*; an important new departure was the creation of the metropolitan counties, based upon the major cities. A serious problem however, was to decide the real extent of these conurbations. It was clearly not sufficient merely to draw a line around the continuous built-up area, because the influence of a conurbation centred upon a major city (such as Manchester for example) extends further than this. Commuters, for instance, often live in dormitory villages which, on the face of it, seem to be outside the conurbation; however, these people make up the bulk of the village population and depend on the conurbation for their work, shopping and entertainment. The dormitory village, therefore, is in many ways a part of the conurbation and ought to be part of the metropolitan county for the purpose of efficient administration and planning.

In fact 'the metropolitan authorities had boundaries which most commentators have regarded as too tightly-drawn, thus infringing the city – hinterland principle' (House *et al*, 1973 p. 25). One reason for this which is not without significance is that many dormitory-village dwellers themselves did not wish to be reorganised into a part of a vast metropolitan area; they wished to hang on to their countryside existence and status. Several areas fought the proposals, Poynton (see figure 2.3) for one winning a reprieve, and remaining in Cheshire on the grounds that its regional centre was Macclesfield (which was also to remain in Cheshire).

The following example resulted from the establishment of the metropolitan county of Greater Manchester, and shows that the boundaries of administrative regions can sometimes appear nonsensical to people because of their insensitivity to local conditions. The maps (figure 2.3) show the county boundaries in the southeast Manchester and northeast Cheshire area before and after reorganisation, as well as the relief, major roads and built-up areas. We shall use the maps to examine the organisation of both secondary education and the Girl Guides' movement in the area. Education, it should be remembered, is administered by local education authorities (the counties and metropolitan districts), whilst the Guides are administered on a county basis, each county being split up into 'divisions' and small 'districts'.

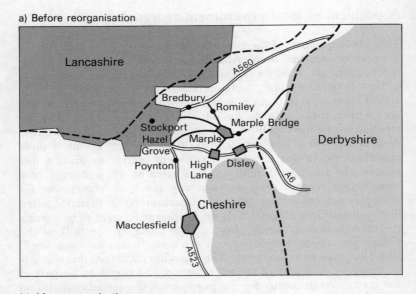

a) Before reorganisation

b) After reorganisation

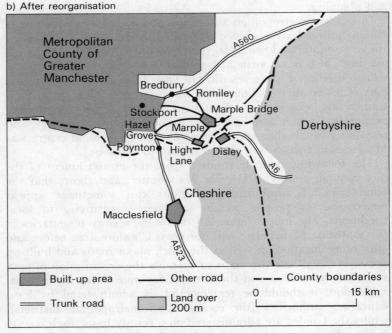

| Built-up area | Other road | County boundaries |
| Trunk road | Land over 200 m | 0   15 km |

Figure 2.3   Southeast Manchester and northeast Cheshire: changing political boundaries

1. Suggest one reason why the Girl Guides, a national youth organisation, should adopt the counties for its broad organisational structure.

2. Make a sketch of figure 2.3(a):
   (a) On this map draw the approximate 'catchment area' for the two Marple secondary schools before reorganisation. It included Disley, High Lane, Hazel Grove, Romiley, Bredbury and Marple Bridge.
   (b) In a different colour draw the approximate divisional boundary for the 'Chadkirk Guides' which includes the following districts: High Lane, Romiley, Bredbury and Woodley, Marple Bridge and Disley.
   (c) Describe and account for the similarities between the secondary schools' catchment area and the boundary of the Chadkirk division of the Girl Guides.

3. Make a sektch of figure 2.3(b):
   (a) Draw the old secondary schools' catchment area, and list the locations that no longer remain within the Cheshire Education Authority. The locations in this list are, of course, also Guide districts that no longer belong in the Cheshire Girl Guides.
   (b) Outline the administrative problems that now exist in Disley from the point of view of Cheshire Education Authority and Cheshire Girl Guides.

4. Briefly describe the possible solutions to these problems (bearing in mind that the nearest administrative centre to Disley which is in Cheshire, is Macclesfield to the south).

Discussion

Had Marple and surrounding locations remained in Cheshire the problems you have been examining would not have arisen. However, for Marple to remain in Cheshire would have been unthinkable because, for reasons of service provision and commuting patterns, it was clearly part of Greater Manchester.

Thus, Disley found itself in a difficult position. Historically, it had looked toward Marple as the local centre for secondary schooling and also for divisional administration in the Girl Guides. After reorganisation Disley was forced to look to the south toward Macclesfield; however, historical and even physical factors worked against this as a practical alternative.

The measures that have been adopted to resolve these problems are as follows. Cheshire Education Authority now has a special arrangement with Stockport Education Authority (that is, the metropolitan district into which Marple now falls) whereby Disley pupils are bussed into Marple. This solves Cheshire's problem of supplying secondary education to an isolated part of the county and, incidentally, solves Stockport's problem of having too many schools in Marple. As from April 1980 the Girl Guides have decided to organise their divisions *across* the county boundaries as this makes more sense from a *local* administrative point of view. Disley district has now been formed into one of the Stockport divisions along the A6 trunk road together with High Lane and Hazel Grove (administered not from Cheshire but from Stockport). The old Chadkirk division now includes Marple Bridge, Bredbury, Woodley and Romiley, Marple being considered large enough to form a division on its own. As a final point it may be added that although this solves the administration problems for Disley it is only a compromise solution; if Disley requires any local government money for camp training or whatever, it still has to apply to Cheshire!

Key issues

BOUNDARIES Boundaries around man-made regions have great significance. Even when people can cross freely from one region to another, the location of boundaries has great importance. It may mean, for example, that a town has no casinos, as in the picture on page 62, or no public houses (as in the case of Letchworth).

SOCIALLY-MADE REGION These are created as an aid to organisation – most activities are organised spatially, from newspaper delivery rounds and police officers' beats to school catchment areas. The United Kingdom is administered through many different types of these regions: countries (England, Scotland, Wales), countries, districts, Regional Health Authorities, development areas, to name just a few.

SPATIAL SCALES Different regions operate at different scales. The size of the area depends in the main upon the purpose of the region. In answer to the question posed about table 2.1, we expect *large* water authorities simply because they have to deal with large catchment areas and river systems.

OVERLAPPING BOUNDARIES Different regions, designed for different purposes, will often have different boundaries. Such overlaps may also occur as regions change over time.

CHANGING BOUNDARIES Many phenomena change over time; populations migrate, settlements grow or decline, and their spheres of influence expand with increasing mobility. In each case, boundaries must be adjusted to take these into account.

3
Perceptual regions and mental maps

.1 Perception

In the previous chapter we concentrated upon the ways in which administrators draw up their regions. In this section we will consider how the users of regions actually *perceive* them – in other words what they make of the world about them.

Let us start with a very simple example. Figure 3.1 illustrates the circulation of local newspapers in an area around York. There are three different journals; one is published in York, one in Malton to the north and one in Selby to the south, and the map shows the villages in which a majority of the people interviewed take one of the three. As we would expect, the size of the catchments for the three settlements corresponds to their size and centrality. York is the largest centre, and its newspaper has the widest circulation. Selby and Malton are far smaller, and their newspapers' circulations reflect this.

If we were discussing *shopping* behaviour, we could explain the fact that people owe allegiance to particular centres in terms of straightforward economic principles. We could, for example, apply Reilly's Law to predict where the catchment boundaries should be drawn around York (see the Appendix on page 66). In this example, of course, central place ideas are not necessarily very useful; newspapers are sold widely, and delivered to the home. People will therefore read a particular paper only if it interests them, or if it has news which they think relates to them. This means that in Cawood (to the south of the map) residents are interested in Selby news, whilst in nearby Riccall, people are more interested in York news.

Newspaper circulation is an indication of people's PERCEPTIONS about an area. What causes these perceptions to differ? The following extract (Pocock and Hudson 1978, pp. 28–9) outlines some of the influences that affect our perceptions:

> The stable cultural characteristics producing a personal response include the individual's personality attributes, attitudes, social class, age, sex and so on. Of these, attitudes is perhaps the most

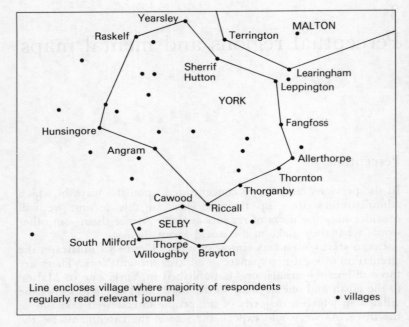

Figure 3.1   *Newspaper circulation around York, Malton and Selby*

important element conditioning perception. This is evident if attitude is interpreted as the summary of past experiences or perceptions . . . nothing is approached in a state of innocence.

Places, then, are seen through acquired cultural filters of standards, expectations, and so on, an approach tantamount to 'believing is seeing', rather than the reverse, 'seeing is believing'.

The last component at the perceiving stage . . . relates to particularity of circumstance, to the needs or moods of the moment, emotional involvement or physical or biogenic needs. Places, as well as people, are quite clearly perceived differently through 'rose coloured spectacles' compared with a 'jaundiced eye' or even a 'Monday morning feeling', for instance. Haste, anger, hunger, illness – all highly colour the response to a particular environment, particularly if it is an individual's first, last or only contact.

In summary, then, perception is a process far from being solely a mechanical response. It is very much a cultural and subjective process, a continuous tuning in, amplification, suppression and interpretation of the observed world.

This extract suggests that we each possess an IMAGE of our immediate environment, and that this image will vary as a result of our upbringing, our background, our age and so on. Let us try to relate this information to the example in figure 3.1

1. What factors will condition the regular purchase of a particular local newspaper?

2. What factors will condition an individual's allegiance to a particular town or city? (You might find it useful here to consult Tidswell's book *Pattern and Process in Human Geography*, pp. 221–33 for details of the shopping patterns in an adjacent area.)

3. Is it likely that everyone living around York, Selby and Malton will have a similar image of these places? What factors might influence this? Remember that this is a rural area, in which transport problems (such as infrequent and expensive bus services) may exist.

Discussion

This simple example illustrates that individual perceptions may condition behaviour, and that these must be taken into account when we are trying to understand spatial activities. In this case, there are clearly-perceived functional regions existing around settlements. It would be very interesting to test how closely 'regional images' correspond to these actual patterns of shopping and recreational behaviour, and then to find out whether people's perceptions dictate their shopping trips, or whether frequent trips to a place cause them to have a favourable image of it.

.2 Barriers to perception

In the last example, it was suggested that different groups might have different images of the world; more specifically, people without cars might perceive different FUNCTIONAL REGIONS than those who are more mobile. We can describe this in another way, and say that different groups have different MENTAL MAPS of an area.

In figure 3.1 we used indirect evidence to find out about images. We can however do this more directly, by asking people to provide us with their mental maps. A simple example will demonstrate the possibilities. If each member of a class is asked to draw a map of the school, the resulting efforts will be very different – the boys, for example, might record the boys' toilets, the girls probably would not! Similarly, the music room or the gymnasium will feature in some pupils' recollections, but not in others.

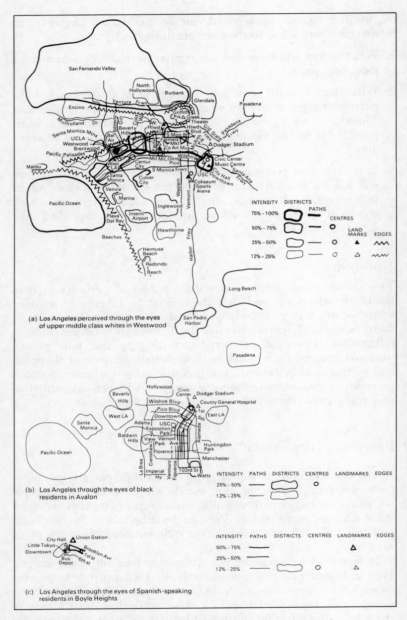

(a) Los Angeles perceived through the eyes of upper middle class whites in Westwood

(b) Los Angeles through the eyes of black residents in Avalon

(c) Los Angeles through the eyes of Spanish-speaking residents in Boyle Heights

Figure 3.2   Mental maps of Los Angeles residents

This may seem a trivial illustration, but in figure 3.2 we can see that images of the environment can vary enormously. In figure 3.2(a), white residents in Los Angeles have provided their mental maps of the city, and their perceptions have been accumulated. Clearly, they are mobile and aware. In figure 3.2(b) a very different picture emerges. This represents the images drawn by blacks, many of whom will be low-income residents, perhaps without cars, and probably relatively immobile. Their knowledge of the city is constrained to a few key landmarks, like the Pacific, Hollywood, the county hospital and Beverly Hills. They do however have a detailed knowledge of the 'downtown' ghetto in which they live whereas this area is *terra incognita* as far as the wealthy whites are concerned. The third map (figure 3.2(c)) takes this argument even further, for it shows the image of Los Angeles perceived by Spanish-speaking immigrants. Here, the known area is tiny; simply the bus depot (through which they probably arrived), city hall (through which they deal with officials) and a few streets in the downtown centre.

3.3 Residential location: where people live

The Los Angeles example shows very clearly that different groups within a city have different images of their environment, and that racial and economic factors are responsible for this diversity. This finding has several implications. One is that individuals with a very limited knowledge of an area will be very constrained in terms of their behaviour. For example, if a black resident of Los Angeles sees a job advertisement for work based at the International Airport (see figure 3.2(a)) he or she may not apply simply because it is part of the city with which they are unfamiliar. In other words, knowledge of a place can be a cumulative process, with individuals who only know the inner city tending to look for work in the same area.

Another thing to emerge from this, and other studies, is that people have definite images of the desirability of neighbourhoods. For example, the white residents all seem to know about the high-status suburbs of Beverly Hills and Bel Air; they do not bother to include the black ghetto areas on their mental maps. These preferences for certain locations are found in any town or city, and have a great deal to do with the way in which people decide where they want to live in a city.

When we examine the residential location process, we have to take into account the housing market; for example, whether a neighbourhood contains private housing or council housing, houses or flats, old properties or new properties. However, within this framework the *image* of the neighbourhood will be important. In some towns and cities, old areas are popular; in other cities they are run-down. In some places flats are keenly sought; in others they are unpopular. This can be tested quite easily:

1. Take a street map of the local area, or that part of the city with which you are familiar. Divide it up into neighbourhoods, taking into account what we have said about the problems of creating regions; aim to draw up at least half-a-dozen areas.

2. Transfer your findings to a simple sketch-map, and then rank the areas that are displayed. Choose the residential area that you think is most desirable, and rank it '1', the next '2' and so on. It may be helpful to combine the class's scores (averaging out all the different ranks), and perhaps to repeat the experiment with parents and teachers.

3. At this point, you should now have a map, with all the neighbourhoods ranked in terms of residential desirability. We can now test this ranking, using data on house prices. These can be collected from estate agents, who usually have a wide range of leaflets describing many types of property. Try to collect a sample of leaflets for fairly similar types of property, and assign the prices to the relevant neighbourhoods. Again, produce an average price (for something like a three-bedroomed semi-detached house) for each neighbourhood, and rank these average prices; the higher the price, the more desirable the neighbourhood.

4. We now have a rank list of perceptions of the residential environment, and an objective rank list of the prices that people are prepared to pay to live in different areas. We can compare the two using Spearman's rank correlation coefficient:

$$r_s = 1 - \frac{6\Sigma \mid (r_1 - r_2)^2 \mid}{(n^3 - n)}$$

This calculation gives us a value ranging from -1 to $+1$ which can be calculated as a normal correlation coefficient. The nearer the r_s value is to 1, the closer the correspondence between the ranks (see the Appendix on page 66).

5. What do the results show? Hopefully, there should be a high r_s value, indicating that your preferences are generally shared by people buying homes. If they are not (that is, if r_s is low) you should compare the ranks, and see which neighbourhoods differ. Try to explain the differences by compiling a list of the factors that influenced your decision. Was peace and quiet important, or the distribution of leisure facilities? Good public transport links, or good views? Is it possible that age is a factor here? Compare your rankings (using r_s) with those of parents and teachers.

Figure 3.3   A mental map of Great Britain. Isolines join locations of equal attraction: high values are the most desirable

Ex-minister says Inmos agreed to back assisted areas

By Kenneth Owen
Technology Editor

Controversy over the decision by the National Enterprise Board's Inmos microelectronics subsidiary to locate its first factory in Bristol will be intensified when Parliament reassembles next week.

Mr Alan Williams, MP for Swansea West who was Minister of State at the Department of Industry under the last Labour Government, intends to mobilize the regional groups of Labour MPs representing Scotland and north-east and north-west England to join him and his south Wales group in protesting at the choice.

There is a conflict between Mr Williams' account of Department of Industry negotiations with Inmos during his time as a government minister and that given by the company.

Mr Williams insists that Inmos gave an undertaking to locate its first two factories in an assisted area or areas. Mr Iann Barron, executive director of Inmos, denied any such agreement.

Mr Williams said that, as Minister of State, he had refused three times to grant an industrial development certificate to Inmos for the company's technology centre to be located at Bristol.

This is the Inmos research and development unit in the United Kingdom, and Bristol was confirmed as its location in December, 1978.

An industrial development certificate for the technology centre, Mr Williams said, was granted only when Inmos gave an undertaking that at least the first two of its production units would be located in assisted areas. Four such areas were envisaged each of which was to employ about 1,000 people.

An Inmos spokesman repeated at the weekend the declaration by Mr. Iann Barron when announcing the choice of Bristol for the first production unit last

month that no such pledge had been made by the company.

One sentence concerning Inmos in the National Enterprise Board's annual report for 1978 said: "The firm intention is that the United Kingdom production facilities will be located in assisted areas." This represented the view of the NEB and not of Inmos, said the company spokesman.

According to Mr Williams, the Inmos undertaking is documented in the records of the Department of Industry and the decision to grant an industrial development certificate for the Bristol technology centre on the basis of that undertaking was taken by collective government decision.

According to Inmos, more than 200 sites were evaluated in a survey by PA Management Consultants before Bristol was chosen for the first production unit. Three areas emerged in the final short-list of five sites—the north-east, south Wales, and the south-west.

Inmos had wanted a prestige site, the company spokesman said, not one "in the middle of a run-down industrial estate". It also made sense to have the research/development and production technologists close together because the company hoped the two groups would mix— "We need the transfer of knowledge both ways".

Thus Inmos plans to combine the production unit with its technology centre to create what it describes as "an integrated capability".

The Inmos plan to set up the Bristol factory is dependent on three main decisions for its realization. It will need an industrial development certificate; planning permission from the North Avon District Council; and approval from Sir Keith Joseph, Secretary of State for Industry, for the NEB-approved second £25m investment in Inmos.

Figure 3.4   Public responses to a plan to relocate industry

Discussion

This example should have revealed that residential preferences are reflected in the prices that people are prepared to pay for houses. (It is also the case that there are desirable and undesirable areas of council housing, and tenants will often wait for long periods to transfer their tenancies to these desirable neighbourhoods.) Nor does this only apply within particular cities; it is also true for the country at large. It would be possible to repeat the above exercise, using instead all the counties in Britain. The rankings that emerged would then indicate the desirable regions within the country. This experiment has been carried out by several researchers, with fairly consistent results (see figure 3.3). These findings are flamboyantly described by Gould and White (1974, p. 83) below — remember that high ranks are being given to desirable locations:

> Using somewhat Bunyanesque terms, the Southern Plateau of Desire is very prominent, and extending from it the East Anglian and Welsh Border Prongs define the now well-known Midland Mental Cirque. In the Southeast the Metropolitan Sinkhole can be easily distinguished, while the highest gradient by far is over the Bristol Channel between England and Wales. Once past the Midlands, the surface falls quite smoothly and regularly, except for the intrusion of the Lake District Dome. In Scotland, where generally low values prevail, the Highlands do a little better than the rest, the exception being a small knoll immediately round the capital at Edinburgh.

Peter Gould and Rodney White found that most people prefer their home area; again, the familiar is being contrasted with the unfamiliar. However, this apart, there is a general agreement on the desirability of the south (except for London) and the undesirability of the north (except for the Lake District).

Do you agree?

.4 Residential location: where people work

Although your views may not correspond to the ones outlined above, there is evidence that they are generally shared by people making decisions about where they want to live and work. Figure 3.4, for example, shows clearly that industrialists are reluctant to locate in so-called undesirable areas.

This is borne out by David Keeble (1976), who has examined changes in employment in Britain over recent years. He notes (p. 288) that the most successful areas (in employment terms) are also the ones generally deemed to be the most attractive:

The 'image' of particular localities as attractive residential environments is now ... a factor of major importance in manufacturing growth, strongly influencing the locational decisions of both workers and industrialists. The implications of this for both regional policy and regional planning, in terms of the need to rehabilitate the urban and industrial environments of the older peripheral manufacturing areas, the problems posed for decaying inner city areas of London or Birmingham, and the growing pressures on attractive rural, coastal or small town locations, are going to require very close attention during the remaining decades of the twentieth century.

1. Relate David Keeble's remarks to the maps of the Assisted Areas displayed in Chapter 2. To what extent do you think the economic problems of these regions have actually been created by their poor environment which makes it hard for them to attract new industry?

2. To what extent can this image be overcome? Can people's images be easily changed?

Key issues

PERCEPTION People perceive things in different ways; eye-witnesses to an accident rarely agree. Different people emphasise different aspects about a place, and their perceptions will thus depend upon whether they are interested in shopping opportunities, recreation or employment.

IMAGE The way in which people perceive something constitutes their image of it. Try to find in newspapers examples of towns trying to improve their image by emphasising what they think are their better points (such as leisure and retailing facilities).

MENTAL MAPS From our images of places we can create mental maps, which complement normal maps based on actual measurement.

FUNCTIONAL REGIONS We have contrasted images with functional regions – such as those created by a system of central places (cities, towns and villages). The functional region around each centre is the area that it serves. However, individual perceptions and preferences may cause some people to use other centres instead. Functional regions are also sometimes called *nodal*, because they exist in relation to a core or node at the centre.

4
Drawing boundaries

So far we have been considering spatial classification in its various forms and at varying scales. Spatial classification, remember, manifests itself as regions on a map. Sometimes regions are even evident to us on the ground; we can actually see them. Examples of such regions would include the 'moorland edge' where arable farming and improved pasture quite abruptly stops, leaving open moorland occupying the higher levels and hill tops. Most regions however are not so clear-cut, and in order to identify a boundary we may have to take into account perceptions and images, as we showed in Chapter 3. How we then draw the boundary will of course depend upon the function of the region. Administrative regions have to be rigorously defined: if we are drawing-up the boundary between two countries, we have to be much more precise than if we are simply attempting to isolate the urban/rural fringe as part of an academic study. Nor is this simply true of frontiers. Imagine the problems that would be caused if countries like Britain and Norway did not have absolutely definite boundaries governing fishing and mineral rights within the North Sea.

In this section a number of simple examples are given in which the difficulties involved in actually drawing the boundaries are highlighted. The examples selected use different scales. We shall begin by considering what are probably the most obvious spatial divisions, namely international boundaries.

.1 National and international boundaries

International frontiers can be seen in any atlas. What an atlas does not usually show, however, is why frontiers are where they are or how often they shift or change. Here an old atlas may be very useful. We have already seen (Chapter 2) how the intra-national boundaries in Britain were changed in 1974, and how this was accompanied by several name changes; Teesside, for example, became Cleveland. We can now assume that this pattern of regions and their names will be stable and long-lasting; especially when we remember that the principle behind local government reorganis-

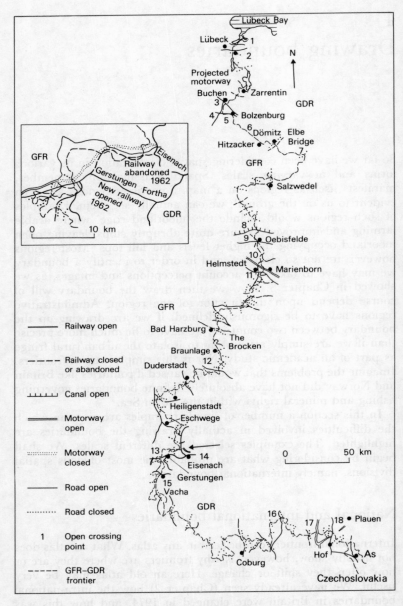

Figure 4.1　Severed transport links across the East-West border in Germany. (For discussion of the insert, see page 37)

---

ation was to bring the regional boundaries into line with the distribution of population.

Using an old atlas in conjunction with a modern map of the world's international boundaries, you might conclude that boundaries have, in some continents, been remarkably stable. In some continents such as Africa and Europe, however, this has not been the case. In the latter, nations like Germany and Italy did not even exist until the last quarter of the nineteenth century, and Germany especially has had constantly fluctuating boundaries both on its western and eastern flanks. Indeed, historians have argued that it was the insensitivity of the Versailles Treaty in 1919, and the effects that this had on the country's western frontiers, that contributed strongly to the outbreak of the Second World War.

Germany's position at the end of that war meant that the country was partitioned, and a new, totally artificial frontier was created on the eastern flank between what is now the Federal Republic and the Democratic Republic. In its own way this solution is even more insensitive, and as figure 4.1 shows, the fortified frontier has severed many natural east-west transport links. One geographer (Mellor, 1978, pp. 138–40) writes:

> The inter-German frontier has become one of the most jealously guarded and tender in Europe, but its disruptive influence in Germany has been exceedingly great. What has become an international division originated as a boundary for administrative convenience between the Soviet and Anglo-American occupation zones, merely to define territorial responsibility of the occupying powers. It was therefore hastily defined using pre-existing local government boundaries, simplified in a few places to make administration easier, but it took no consideration whatsoever of the economic and human landscape, disregarding land ownership and communications.
>
> The impact of the new frontier has been particularly harsh in the richer Börde country, cutting across the main east–west lines of movement between Magdeburg and Braunschweig. South of Helmstedt, the frontier disrupts several brown-coal-mines, while a new power station had to be built at Offleben on the western side to compensate for current formerly supplied from the GDR Harbke power station. Another complex problem in the area around Bebra and Eisenach arises from the frontier crossing and recrossing main railways and roads, so that the GDR built a new section of railway entirely within its own territory. The Eckertal dam near Bad Harzburg is bisected by the frontier with a barrier erected on the demarcation line halfway across, so hampering maintenance and operation.

Major disruption by the new frontier of closely knit textile, glass, and porcelain industries has occurred in the Upper Franconian and the Saxony–Thuringian industrial area, where the Coburg district has been cut from its usual railway access to North Germany and the Lower Rhine, requiring now a much longer and correspondingly more expensive journey. In Landkreis Kronach, Bavaria, the railway connection of the Tettau glass and porcelain industry has been cut by the new frontier and up to ten wagonloads daily have to be brought over 10 km on road rollers from the station at Steinbach-am-Wald, the additional costs being carried by the Federation. The brewery at Falkenstein, also in Landkreis Kronach, has lost 90 per cent of its market area by the new frontier cutting it from Thuringia. On the eastern side of the border, the small and once prosperous resort of Blankenstein now has no tourist traffic because it lies in the 500 m protective zone along the frontier. In all the new frontier has closed 32 railway crossings, 3 motorway crossings, 31 main highways, and over 140 other roads, besides innumerable tracks and paths. There remain open 8 railways, 5 roads and motorways, the Mittelland Canal and the Elbe.

Whilst Germany is perhaps an extreme example, it is by no means the only case of this kind within the Continent. Considering Europe as a whole, the following simple questions should be answered:

1. From within Europe, find three examples of international boundaries that:
   (*a*) Do not have any readily apparent physical basis and have been unstable during the last 50 years.
   (*b*) Do seem to have a physical basis, and have been stable.
   (*c*) Do not fall into either category (a) or (b).

2. Try to identify reasons why the examples you have chosen for (a) above are unstable. For this you may have to resort to other maps that show more information than the nations and their boundaries.

3. Why is it that the countries chosen for (b) above have very stable international frontiers?

Discussion

This section illustrates once again that boundaries between regions, or more precisely in this case, nations, are political and are capable of change. But what is the rationale behind these particular lines on the map? Clearly some international boundaries divide peoples with sharp cultural differences, perhaps language differences, or even mutual hostility. But this is not always the case, and sometimes boundaries seem to sweep across territory with no regard for CULTURAL or linguistic factors. Switzerland, a remarkably stable nation, has people of three linguistic groups, for example. A far larger example is that of the Soviet Union, which has within its nineteen republics an enormous diversity of races and religions; for instance, it has one of the largest Islamic populations in the world.

If there exists a degree of similarity, of cultural homogeneity, a nation can ensure great stability on its frontiers if it exploits a natural feature of major significance in the landscape. A range of mountains such as the Pyrenees between France and Spain is such an example; it not only reduces the amount of movement and interaction between the nations (thus literally 'dividing' the nations), but also offers a defensive barrier. The defensive importance of the English Channel to Britain has often been demonstrated in past wars, ensuring that Britain's frontier has not been violated in recent history.

When a 'natural' frontier does not exist, artificial international boundaries can be unstable, even when there is some cultural justification for their existence. The boundary between Germany, France, and the Benelux countries (even where it follows the Rhine, a natural barrier) has been notoriously unstable; one important reason for this is that there has invariably been pressure for the frontier to shift in favour of one nation against the others, usually as a result of valuable minerals lying just beyond or across a frontier. In 1919, as we have already suggested, this pressure was at the expense of Germany.

Of course, when a frontier has no physical basis and also cuts across cultural similarities, that frontier may be disputed. Sometimes a single cultural group can be alienated by a boundary that has been drawn without their particular interests in mind, as Northern Ireland will testify. However, it is in the continent of Africa that this is most clearly demonstrated. During the nineteenth and twentieth centuries, the imperial powers imposed an entirely new, and frequently artificial, set of frontiers upon the existing tribal divisions. The result of this mismatch has been described in the following terms (*National Geographical Magazine*, February 1980):

> What proved disastrous was the imposition of foreign political systems and arbitrary boundaries which often divided language and cultural groups. The resulting ethnic fragmentation has helped touch off some fifty successful coups during the post-independence period.

We will examine such instability in Book 2, *Interaction*.

4.2 A cultural–linguistic divide in Wales

Following our brief look at the nature of international boundaries we can trace a similar theme, namely the drawing of divides between different cultural or linguistic groups. We shall investigate a regional pattern which has no political, economic or administrative meaning today, but remains a real cultural division vivid enough to allow us to recognise a regional boundary. The cultural divide in question is known as the 'Pembrokeshire Landsker' (Pembrokeshire is now part of the county of Dyfed) and as B. S. John (1972) has written 'there can be few administrative units in the British Isles which present linguistic features as fascinating as those of Pembrokeshire. These features are related largely to the presence of the Landsker, an ancient frontier which has been a marked linguistic and cultural divide between north and south Pembrokeshire for almost a thousand years.'

The Normans who colonised and unified much of Britain

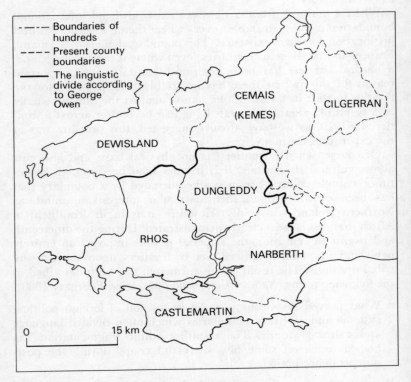

Figure 4.2   a) The Landsker in Pembrokeshire 1603

imposed an unprecedented administrative structure. The Landsker in Norman times really formed the administrative frontier between the more fertile, lowland southern Pembrokeshire and the poorer northern territory held by the native Celts. The Landsker persisted long after the need for a military frontier had gone and is known to have been an important linguistic and cultural divide in Elizabethan times. In the nineteenth century it was written that there was very little interaction between the two 'ethnic' groups and that the boundary was still stable. By the Second World War, however, it was reported that English-biased education (and radio and in turn television) had tended to blur the ancient boundary.

We can attempt to judge whether a linguistic divide does exist (and particularly whether we are able to draw a boundary to show the Landsker on a map) by considering both CENSUS data and information arising from fieldwork.

Examine the maps, figures 4.2(a), (b), (c). Figure 4.2(a) shows the Landsker in 1603, the Welsh-speaking part north of the line and

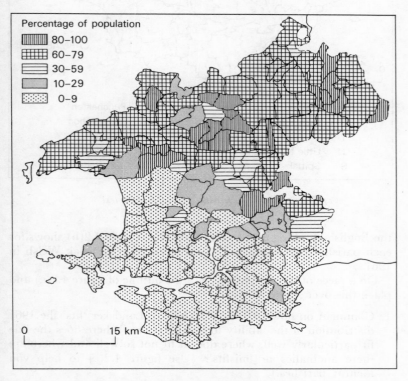

b) The distribution of the Welsh-speaking population in 1961

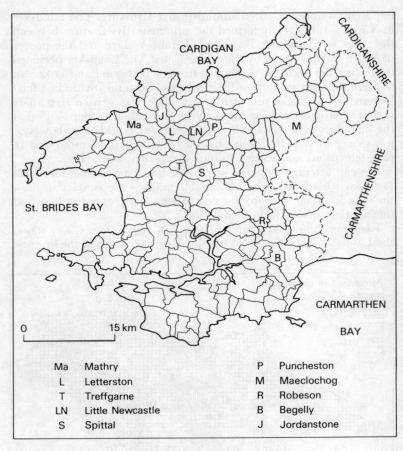

Ma   Mathry   P   Puncheston
 L   Letterston   M   Maeclochog
 T   Treffgarne   R   Robeson
LN   Little Newcastle   B   Begelly
 S   Spittal   J   Jordanstone

c) The distribution of parishes referred to in the text

the English-speaking part south of the line. Figure 4.2(b) shows for each parish the percentages of population able to speak Welsh in 1961.

On a piece of tracing paper, trace the outline of figure 4.2(a) and place this over figure 4.2(b).

1. Comment on how well the Elizabethan Landsker 'fits' the 1961 distribution of the 'ability to speak Welsh'. Where does the line fit particularly well, where does it fit not so well and where are there anomalies or 'misfits'? (Use figure 4.2(c) to help you identify parishes.)

2. Can you offer any explanation for the anomalies? An atlas map of Pembrokeshire might help you here.

3. Does the evidence shown in figure 4.2(b) enable us to draw a boundary for a present-day Landsker, that really divides north and south Pembrokeshire? If you think it is possible, attempt to draw the line on your tracing overlay; but in any event, give reasons for your answer.

4. You may feel that there are weaknesses in the census information. Identify ways in which the census data may be misleading; to give you a hint, it may be that the census data *underestimate* the real strength of Welsh in some parishes, but *overestimate* the real strength of Welsh in others.

5. How could these weaknesses in the census be overcome?

Discussion

There is clearly a relationship between the 1603 Landsker and the map showing 1961 census results. However you will probably have noted that the relationship is far from perfect; the divide between English and Welsh speakers in 1961 is not as abrupt as the Elizabethan Landsker indicates that it once was, and there are parishes to the north of the old Landsker that cannot be described as Welsh-speaking. No doubt the spread of English influences accounts for the latter, and it is interesting that many of the northern parishes of relatively few Welsh speakers are on or near the main north–south road.

English influences are various, ranging from the gradual encroachment of English-based secondary education to the occupation of rural housing for second or retirement homes. It would appear that although in some places the divide between 'Welshness' and 'Englishness' is abrupt (for example, in the west between Haycastle and Camrose), it is far more a 'zone of transition' in its central part (for example, from the parish of Uzmaston to the north, northeast and east). This means that, in the central section at least, it would be very difficult to decide the exact position of a boundary.

A possible cause for this confusion could well be that the information in figure 4.2(b) is not really precise enough. To begin with, it does not tell us about the ability to read or write Welsh, which would be a better measure of how Welsh a person is. More important though, is the actual usage of the language; a person in Haverfordwest, for instance, might be able to speak Welsh but this does not mean to say that (s)he ever uses it. On the other hand a

person in the parish of New Moat (just north of the medieval Landsker) might well only use English when (s)he has to; in *all* other
family or business transactions (s)he would use Welsh. In the
absence of any secondary information – that is, figures or docu-
mentary sources of any kind – the only way around this problem
is fieldwork; a survey must be carried out to assess directly the
usage of the Welsh language.

Fieldwork

The aim of this fieldwork, carried out by some sixth-formers in
1979, was to assess how meaningful the Landsker is today, to test
the strength of the cultural (linguistic) differences between north
and south Pembrokeshire and to try to identify whether the divide
is a clear-cut line or more a zone of transition. The practical difficulties were great; the size of the area under consideration is large
and the number of students involved relatively small, which meant
that transport problems were major. The number of people interviewed, therefore, was not large, but enough for the results to be
of interest (the total sample size was 121). Pairs of students interviewed people in both villages and isolated farmhouses within their
assigned area of Pembrokeshire, and the questions asked were:

1. Can you speak Welsh?

2. (If you answered 'yes' to question 1) Do you *normally* speak
   Welsh in the home?

3. Have you heard of the Landsker?

4. If you think there is a divide between a 'more English' and a
   'more Welsh' part of Pembrokeshire, in which part do you
   consider yourself to be?

There is no room here to give a complete analysis of the results,
but a summary of them is presented on the map below (figure 4.3)
and in the following concluding comment, both taken from the field
report written by one of the students involved:

> It is evident that there is indeed a very definite divide between
> a Welsh area in the north and an English area in the south, with
> a transitional zone between the two extremes which was very
> wide in places . . . It was clear that the Welsh-speaking people
> answering 'yes' to question 2 were mostly of an older age group
> and that comparatively few of the younger generation (that is,
> below 25 years old) chose to speak Welsh, normally.
>
> This, looking at figure 4.3, could be particularly the case in
> the central section towards Fishguard. In Little Newcastle for

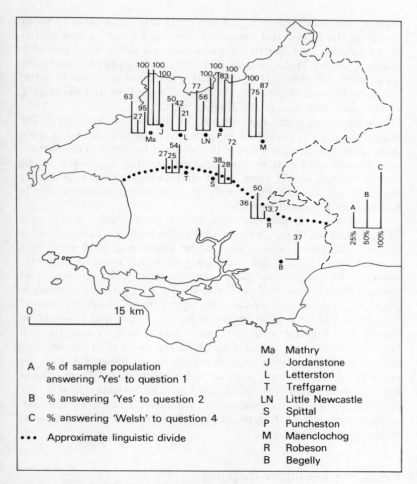

Figure 4.3   The linguistic divide and fieldwork results, 1979

example, although 77.5 per cent of the people questioned were able to speak Welsh, only about half of these normally spoke Welsh in the home.

The students were asked to draw a Landsker line on a base map using fieldwork and census evidence and an approximate boundary is shown in figure 4.3. Treffgarne and Spittal (in the zone of transition according to the census data alone) have been placed firmly in the English half (although the cautious comment of the student quoted earlier is clearly justified). There is in Spittal, for example, a minority of people who claim the ability to speak Welsh and of these a very small minority (28 per cent) say they normally speak Welsh in the home. Robestone, on the other hand, is still placed in the English part but its circumstances are different; a minority is able to speak Welsh, but of these 50 per cent say they normally speak it in the home. It is the final question that seems to settle the issue, for both Robestone and Spittal, as substantial majorities, would place *themselves* in the English part.

Bearing in mind the inadequacies of this fieldwork noted at the beginning, does it enable us to draw any conclusions? Apart from those quoted above from one of the students involved in the survey, we can only add that to draw a hard and fast boundary in the middle section would seem to be undesirable unless it is clearly remembered that any line is only an approximation which merely summarises a zone of transition.

It is clearly still possible, even in the present day, to talk of a 'Welsh' and an 'English' part of Pembrokeshire. The boundary between the two would appear to be less strong than in former times and perhaps it is still weakening. As a final thought, however, would it be possible to gauge the strength of the division and whether the division will persist in the future by trying to analyse other aspects of day-to-day life apart from language alone? Education will be a great influence for the future and it would be revealing to investigate both primary and secondary education in Pembrokeshire; both are 'all English' in the south of Pembrokeshire but, north of the approximate divide shown in figure 4.3, the vast majority of schools have at least some teaching in Welsh. Other aspects that might be investigated would include church- (or chapel-) going (and the language in which services are conducted), social activities (or is English-biased television now the major social activity?) and so on.

4.3 Resolving boundary disputes

These examples show how difficult it is to draw up perfect boundaries that satisfy all parties. In this last section, we consider two cases where attempts are being made to resolve these problems. The first involves negotiation, the second an objective statistical approach.

Figure 4.4 reintroduces the theme of artificial boundaries being imposed by colonial administrators. It shows a small area in Ashanti (Ghana), in which a district official called Fell decided upon the frontier between two tribes in 1913. His decision, however, cut across the tribal perceptions, and twenty-eight years later the case came before the Ghanaian courts. The Nkwanta argued that the original frontier was far to the south of Fell's

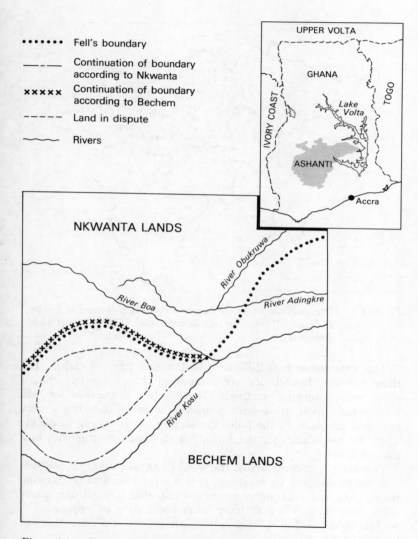

Figure 4.4   Boundary disputes and colonial administration: the Nkwanta and the Bechem (Ghana)

choice. In law, there proved however to be many issues that needed to be taken into account, with the result that the case went to several appeals. Eventually, the boundary was allowed to stand, but only after the court had actually made a close inspection of the area.

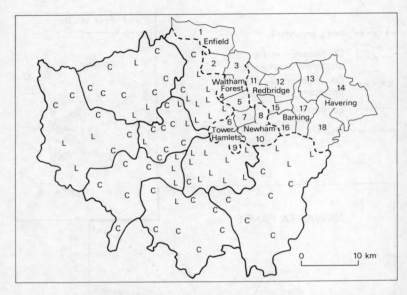

Figure 4.5   *The constituencies for the European Parliament elections in London,*
1979, with Westminster constituencies marked Conservative (C) and
Labour (L)

This case shows how difficult it is to assess different claims. For
these reasons, boundaries are sometimes drawn up by officials
using more objective methods. In this last discussion we will
concentrate upon using such a technique in considering a very
practical problem; in the following section we are going to decide
upon the boundaries for the European election constituencies in a
part of London.

You may have come across the word GERRYMANDERING, without
fully understanding its meaning. It is a term that means 'drawing
boundaries and creating constituencies so that a particular party
wins, even though it may have fewer votes than its opponents'†.
As Johnston (1979, p. 172) says there are several ways that this can
happen:

1. Creating *stacked* districts, of unusual shapes, which seek out
   relatively isolated pockets of the party's support and amal-
   gamates them to produce a seat in which the party has a
   majority.

† The origin of the term 'gerrymander' is illustrative of its meaning. It derives from
a redrawing of constituencies undertaken in Massachussetts by Governor E. Gerry
(1812). One of the long convoluted shapes which resulted from this re-districting
looked like a salamander, and this Gerry-mander has remained in the language
ever since.

Table 4.1 Westminster constituencies and Labour support (1979 election)

Constituency	Labour vote as percentage of turnout
1 Enfield North	41
2 Edmonton	47
3 Chingford	27
4 Walthamstow	50
5 Leyton	51
6 Bethnal Green	50
7 Newham North West	54
8 Newham North East	61
9 Stepney and Poplar	62
10 Newham South	64
11 Wanstead and Woodford	19
12 Ilford North	37
13 Romford	32
14 Upminster	35
15 Ilford South	43
16 Barking	52
17 Dagenham	52
18 Hornchurch	43

2. Creating *packed* districts, by concentrating the opposition party's votes into a very few safe seats, creating a large number of excess votes for them.
3. Creating *cracked* districts, by diluting the opposition voting strengths as a minority in a large number of seats, producing many wasted votes for them.

In simple terms then, gerrymanders can involve connecting very scattered groups of voters, or concentrating your opponents in a small area with enough votes to win the seats many times over, or joining each group of your opponents to just enough of the supporters of the party in power to make sure they lose each time.

Gerrymanders *can* be drawn using trial and error but it is possible to be a great deal more precise, by using statistical methods. In the example below we will employ ANALYSIS OF VARIANCE as a measure of the voting patterns that we create. In figure 4.5 the existing parliamentary constituencies in northeast London are displayed, along with the present European election boundaries; table 4.1 shows the variation in Labour support within the area.

As we can see, figure 4.5 displays two of the large constituencies (each contains approximately half a million voters). One is a

Table 4.2   Analysis of Variance; 1979 European election results

Labour seat	Conservative seat	
41	19	
47	37	
27	32	
50	35	
51	43	
50	52	
54	52	
61	43	
62		
64		
Total (Σ)= 507	Total (Σ)= 313	$\Sigma\Sigma$820
X = 50.7	X = 39.1	
N = 10	N = 8	

Total	ss =	2527
Between	ss =	595
Within	ss =	1932

	ss	DF	
Total	ss = 2527	17	
Between	ss = 595 $\div$	1	= 595
Within	ss = 1932 $\div$	16	= 120.75

$$F\text{-ratio} \frac{(\text{between ss})}{(\text{within ss})} = 4.92$$

Labour seat, the other a Conservative. We can measure the distribution of the Labour vote between the two constituencies as follows. For the analysis of variance, we need three measures, the total sum of squares, the between sum of squares, and the within sum of squares. This gives a clue as to the definition of variance: it is the sum of variations about the mean value of a group of numbers. This will become clear during the calculations shown in Table 4.2 (detailed instructions are given in the Appendix, page 66).

In this example, the 'between sum of squares' is bigger than the 'within ss'; the constituencies, however, are very different, although there is a good deal of variation (variance) of the vote within each seat. The F ratio gives us a single precise measure of these two figures.

In order to gerrymander, we aim for a particular F-*ratio.* Let us try to redraw the boundary between the two constituencies, in order to

Table 4.3   *Analysis of variance; gerrymandered constituencies*

	Labour seat		Conservative seat	
	47		41	
	50		27	
	51		19	
	50		37	
	54		32	
	61		35	
	62		43	
	64		43	
	52			
	52			
Σ =	543	Σ =	227	$\Sigma\Sigma$ 820
X =	54.3	X =	34.6	
N =	10	N =	8	

Total	ss =	2527	
Between	ss =	1720	
Within	ss =	807	

	ss	DF		
Total	ss = 2527	17		
Between	ss = 1720 ÷	1	=	1720
Within	ss = 807 ÷	16	=	50.4
F-ratio			=	34.1

create a *packed* distribution; in other words we will concentrate all the Labour parliamentary seats into one European constituency, so that there are votes which are wasted. This gives us the calculation in Table 4.3.

In this example, the F-ratio is very large, reminding us that the variance between the constituencies is great, while the variation within is very small. In this particular case, Labour wastes votes (winning by ten seats to the Conservatives' eight), which means that the Tories might be able to use that additional support in another part of London.

In both of these examples, Labour and Conservative have each won one European seat. Let us now try to gerrymander so that Labour win both. We will aim for a *stacked* distribution.

1. Remind yourself of the meaning of a stacked distribution.

2. Decide which parliamentary seats will be put together to create the two new Euro-seats.

Table 4.4   Gerrymander for 2–0 Labour win

	Labour seat		Labour seat
	54		50
	61		41
	32		47
	35		27
	43		50
	52		51
	52		62
	43		64
			19
			37
Σ	$\overline{372}$	Σ	$\overline{448}$
X =	46.5	X =	44.8
N =	8	N =	10

Total	ss		
Between	ss		
Within	ss		
	ss	DF	
Total	ss		
Between	ss	÷ 1 =	
Within	ss	÷ 16 =	
F-ratio		=	

3. Work out the *F*-ratio.

As a hint, you want to aim for an *F*-ratio that is as small as possible, in which the within-variance is nearly as high as the between-variance. Only in that way can Labour just win both seats. In table 4.4 we present one solution: work out the *F*-ratio and compare it with yours.

Discussion

Throughout this chapter we have concentrated upon the problems of drawing boundaries. Sometimes these problems have a political basis, and are virtually impossible to resolve. In other cases, they are a reflection of the blurred nature of reality. Our latest example is a reminder of why geographers use quantitative methods: in other words, in order to overcome these imprecisions.

The gerrymandering example is a practical, political one, although it can of course be used in other contexts – even in the

Landsker case, for instance. While we are concentrating on the problems of drawing boundaries, we should not forget to consider the implications of what we have been doing. Just how democratic is a political system in which the election results can be manipulated like this? Do extreme solutions of cracking, stacking and packing occur? Examine the political boundaries in your area, and apply some F-test thinking to them.

Key Issues

CULTURAL We can identify cultural regions on the basis of factors such as religion and language, as opposed to factors such as wealth or race.

CENSUS The Census of Population is taken every decade (the most recent one was taken in 1981). It measures the characteristics of every household in the country.

GERRYMANDERING Gerrymandering involves changing electoral constituency boundaries in order to gain political advantage.

ANALYSIS OF VARIANCE This is a statistical measure that compares the variance within two groups (variance is a precise method of measuring variation about the average), and also the variance between two groups. If the variance between the groups is large, we can usually say that the groups have very different characteristics.

5
Conclusions

The purpose of this book has been to consider in some detail the whole idea of regions. We have tried to say *why* regions are so important despite the fact that the art of regionalisation or spatial classification is particularly difficult. We have examined these difficulties with reference to several different *types* of region and on a number of different *scales*, ranging from the global to the local.

Regions are not, of course, a new idea in geography. In fact, from the time that geography emerged as a subject widely taught and studied (which was effectively only after the Second World War) until fairly recently, regions were undoubtedly *the* central focus. It was the geographer's role to collect information about the world and to classify it so that instructive and descriptive maps could be drawn; such maps would illustrate books describing countries and continents. The nearest we have got to such regions is in section 1.3 'Natural Regions in Geography', and these do fulfil a very important function in helping us understand the world.

By way of a summary of how the idea of regions has developed we can refer to extracts from a recently published discussion between two geographers, P. Whiteley and A. Frey:

P. W. I can see that to keep alive, every subject must change, but surely new things are happening all the time in regions – new ports are opened, and steel works built, population is migrating, towns expanding and so on. Surely regional geography has to keep abreast of events?

A. F. Steel works and new towns and so on form the traditional elements of regional geography which puts the emphasis on inventory, on description, on lists, on characterisation. This traditional form puts the emphasis on fact, rather than the explanation of the fact. It puts the emphasis on what we would call form, that is to say patterns, the distributions, the shapes and the appearance, rather than the processes which give rise to that form.

P. W. But there are different kinds of region that geographers recognise these days.

A. F. You are quite right to draw attention to this, in fact there are indeed three major kinds of region. We have been talking so far of an area picked out because of some unifying quality (such as 'natural regions').

The second type of region we would call nodal, because it focuses on a node or a centre. The area tributary to a city is defined by a number of items, commuter travel or bus services or newspaper circulation or some combination of functions like that.

P. W. What about regions like Australia, Somerset and the parish of Nether Wallop?

A. F. These are the third kind. They are administrative regions in which action of some kind takes place, like planning or collecting refuse.

P. W. Now of the three kinds of regions which you have mentioned, which one is the most important to the geographer?

A. F. Since the last war, the last two have become a lot more important, the nodal region because of the great growth of the cities and the administrative region because of the considerable growth of planning, and because most data come from such regions.

In Chapters 2 and 4 we looked at the type of region that Frey has called the administrative region; we investigated briefly national boundaries in Chapter 4, and in Chapter 2 we examined 'socially-made regions'. With regard to the latter it is interesting to note that during his discussion Frey mentions the practical importance of drawing up regions:

> There are those occasions when new boundaries have to be drawn as in the restructuring of the English county and districts system in 1974. If a firm takes on an extra salesman, it might well have to re-draw the sales territories of its salesmen in order to give them all good earning prospects. The location of facilities such as hospitals and schools is also very much part of the regional problem and we ought to know this from the way in which the government has directed firms to the development areas in recent years.

One type of region that Frey does not mention is the perceptual region which we discussed in Chapter 3. It is most important, however, to realise the significance of the mental images people have, particularly in the light of the final sentence of the quotation immediately above. The 'regional problem' that Frey refers to above is at least in part a perceptual problem based upon people's images of places.

Two recurring themes have been the way regions are defined, and the characteristics of regional boundaries, which are often far from perfect. These topics also entered Frey and Whiteley's discussion:

P. W.   More than once during our conversation you have talked of classification and regionalisation as if they were the same thing. Was this intentional?

A. F.   It was no accident, because the two processes are very similar. Just as you can classify by grouping individuals together by the similarities they have to each other, so you can start at the other end with the whole population or the whole world and split that into sub-groups on the basis of the differences one group has from another. You can do this with parcels of land or regions, just as you can classify anything. The problem is that while core areas may be distinctive enough for any fool to recognise, the boundaries are usually very blurred.

P. W.   Yet regions are not regions unless they have got firm sharp boundaries, surely?

A. F.   In real life we have the dilemma that most regions grade imperceptibly one into another by means of gradual transition zones. Yet academic study and real life purposes of one kind or another require us to draw a firm single line on a map to signify that up to that line you are in Region A, and the other side of that line in Region B. Region A could be an area of dominantly coniferous trees whereas Region B is dominantly deciduous, and a line goes through the zone where the trees are mixed 50–50 coniferous and deciduous. Yet for many purposes it is essential to have a firm line even though one isn't justified.

As a final conclusion, then, we can state that, in many walks of life – from abstract academic research to important practical matters of administrative organisation – spatial classification is necessary. Bearing this in mind we can let Alan Frey have the final word: '. . . regions can never be right or wrong, they can only be useful or convenient, and appropriate or inappropriate for the particular purpose you have in mind.'

Photographic section

1 The Brandenburg Gate, East Berlin

The camera is poised over the border between West and East Berlin, facing south. Immediately beyond the Gate, which now functions as a major checkpoint, is an open area which lies within the DDR (German Democratic Republic); on the horizon lies the district of Kreuzberg, which is within the BRD (Federal Republic of Germany).

In pre-war Berlin, the Brandenburg Gate was a focal point, rather like Marble Arch in London, which straddled the main East-West thoroughfare. This has now been artificially cut by the border, which can be seen looping round the monument; traffic is still channelled by the morphology of the city towards this point – however, the artificial boundary and frontier post severely restrict movement between the two sections of the city.

1. When was the border constructed, and why?

2. Despite its central location, the Gate is not surrounded by other buildings. Why is this?

2 Cutteslowe Wall, Oxford

The photograph shows the wall, taken from the bedroom window of one of the owner-occupied homes. On the other side of the wall can be seen the council houses which were erected in 1932. The home owners were so worried that their suburb's status would be threatened by children playing, noise and refuse from the local authority tenants that they – illegally – built this barrier. It was subsequently knocked down by local authority workmen.

1. Do you think that the wall was a reaction to a real threat or a perceived threat?

2. Local authority tenants may not like living near to home owners (the latter are still more likely to have cars for example, a threat

to pets and young children). Why do owner-occupiers however feel that they have more to lose than tenants?

3. When the wall was demolished, is it likely that the barrier ceased to exist?

3   This is the Place, Utah–Nevada state line

The neon cowboy is immediately beyond the state boundary, on the Nevada side, attracting the attention of traffic on Interstate Highway 80. Motorists who have passed through Utah have driven through a state in which gambling is not permitted; the sign reminds them that they have now arrived in Nevada where gambling is in fact a major dollar earner. Once again therefore we find an artificial boundary – this time a legal rather than a concrete one – which dictates human behaviour.

1. This cowboy is 400 miles from Nevada's most famous gambling centre: what is its name?

2. Utah possesses many prohibitions. What is unique about many of its inhabitants?

3. Can you think of any other examples where inhabitants regularly cross state or national boundaries in order to avail themselves of local advantages they cannot obtain at home?

4   'CORBY WORKS'

This is the enticing title of the widely distributed advertisement seen in the national press during the early 1980s, after the closure of the iron and steel works there. The message is aimed at industrialists and potential industrialists, and it emphasises the unusual circumstances of the town. It is perhaps relevant to remember that the origin of the town itself was unusual; it was established in the 1930s specifically as an iron and steel town utilising local ore deposits, with New Town status.

1. Identify other locations that were also designated as Development Areas *and* steel closure areas.

2. In what ways could Corby be said to be unusual in comparison with these other locations (especially in terms of its location)?

3. There are very few locations that can offer such a wide range of incentives for industry. What *other* advantages does Corby claim to possess over the other Development Areas and the other locations with Enterprise Zones?

5 Advance Factory Units, Milton Keynes New Town

One of the publicity pictures taken by the New Town Development Corporation. The latter is responsible for attracting industry – and inhabitants – to Milton Keynes, and of importance is the creation of the right image. Both industrialists and potential residents are attracted by the garden city ideal, which is heavily stressed in advertisements.

1. From this photograph, identify the response that the MKDC hopes to engender from an industrialist. List the adjectives that would describe this scene.

2. Repeat this exercise in relation to a potential resident. How successful is Milton Keynes? (See Book 3, Chapter 1.)

6 Street Barricade, Londonderry, Ulster

The photograph shows a temporary barricade erected by residents to keep out political and religious opponents, the army and the police. Such borders or frontiers reflect changing population distributions and in times of trouble, residents retreat to 'safe' neighbourhoods.

Londonderry is also an excellent example of the power of the gerrymander. The town was divided into three wards in 1840, and the geography of the city ensured that the protestant minority maintained electoral control right up until 1969. It is perhaps hardly surprising that Londonderry was the centre of civil rights campaigning in the late sixties, and has experienced sporadic communal strife – as witnessed above – since then.

Photograph 1   The Brandenburg Gate, East Berlin

Photograph 2 Cutteslowe Wall, Oxford

Photograph 3   This is the Place. Utah–Nevada state line

Photograph 4 'CORBY WORKS'

Photograph 5   Advance Factory Units, Milton Keynes New Town

Photograph 6   Street Barricade, Londonderry, Ulster

Appendix

1. Reilly's Law of Retail Gravitation may be expressed in various ways: the easiest is:

$$\frac{P_i}{dxi^2} = \frac{P_j}{dxj^2}$$

where P_i and P_j are the two populations of two urban areas, i and j.

x is the breakpoint between i and j
dxi is the distance from i to x
dxj is the distance from j to x

2. The Spearman r_s is calculated as follows:

r_1	r_2	$r_1 - r_2{}^2$
1	4	9
2	1	1
3	3	0
4	1	9

$$\frac{6\Sigma\, r_1 - r_2{}^2}{n^3 - n} = \frac{6 \times 19}{64 - 4}$$

$$r_s = 1 - \frac{114}{60}$$

$$= -0.9$$

If you are familiar with significance tests, values of r_s can be interpreted like any correlation coefficient.

3. Analysis of variance: we work out the sums of squares in the following manner.

   (a) TOTAL SS Square all the values in the two columns ($41\%^2 + 47\%^2$) and sum them. Next, sum all the values; square this total; divide by the number of items (18 in this case). Subtract the latter from the first calculation.

$$\underset{i\ j}{\Sigma\Sigma}\, \chi^{ij2} - \frac{(\underset{i\ j}{\Sigma\Sigma}\, \chi^{ij})^2}{N}$$

   (b) BETWEEN SS Sum the data in column one; square it; divide by N, the number of items; add to similar figure obtained for column two. Subtract the *second* value worked out in *total ss*

$$\frac{\left(\sum_{i} \chi^{i}_{1}\right)^{2}}{N_1} + \frac{\left(\sum_{i} \chi^{i}_{2}\right)^{2}}{N_2} - \frac{\left(\sum_{ij} \chi^{ij}\right)^{2}}{N}$$

(*c*) WITHIN SS If you think about this for a second, you will realise that this must be:

Total ss − Between ss

The only other thing you need to know is *DF*. This stands for degrees of freedom, and can be found as follows:

Total ss: $DF = N - 1$ *where N is the number of items of data*

Between ss: $DF = K - 1$

Within ss: $DF = N - K$ *where K is the number of columns of data*

References

Bradford, M. and Kent, A. (1977) *Human Geography*, Oxford University Press, Oxford.

Dury, G. H. (1978) *The British Isles*, Heinemann, London.

Gould, P. and White R. (1974) *Mental Maps*, Penguin, Harmondsworth.

Haggett, Peter (1975) *Geography: a modern synthesis*, Harper and Row, London.

House, J. (*et al.*) (1973) *The UK Space*, Weidenfeld and Nicholson, London.

John, B. S. (1972) 'The linguistic significance of the Pembrokeshire Landsker', *Pembrokeshire Historian*, **4**, 7–29.

Johnston, R. J. (1979) *Political, Electoral and Spatial Systems*, Oxford University Press, Oxford.

Keeble, D. (1976) *Industrial Location and Planning in the U.K.*, Methuen, London.

Knox, P. (1974) 'Spatial variations in level of living in England and Wales', Institute of British Geographers, *Transactions*, **62**, 1–15.

Mellor, R. H. (1978) *The Two Germanies*, Harper Row, London.

National Geographical Magazine, *Africa: its political development*, **157**, 2 (Feb.) 1980.

Pocock, D. C. and Hudson, R. (1978) *Images of the Urban Environment*, Macmillan, London.

Tidswell, V. (1976) *Pattern and Process in Human Geography*, University Tutorial Press, London.

Whiteley P. and Frey, A. (1979) *Geography*, Sussex Books.

This book is to be returned on or before
the last date stamped below.

KIRBY a LAMBERT   97277